Live Laugh Love

Surayya Kanji

BookLeaf Publishing

Presentation by *BookLeaf Publishing*

Web: www.bookleafpub.com

E-mail: info@bookleafpub.com

ISBN: 9789357617468

First edition 2022

To my amazing partner, for being my biggest supporter but always keeping me grounded.

To my not-so-little brother, for never calling me by my name and for always saying hi on FaceTime.

To my loving parents, for always pushing me and being there for me, even when I push back.

To you, the reader, for picking up this book and letting me share my life with you.

PREFACE

Poetry has always been my go-to medium for expressing myself. I've always dreamed of publishing my writing, and I am so excited (aka nervous) to be able to share my experiences with you, the reader. These twenty one poems are a reflection of my twenty one years of experiences, and a product of the events that have impacted me. So let them engage you, maybe guide you, but definitely inspire you.

My Perfect Life

My perfect life,
Shattered by his strife.
It wasn't his fault,
That he kept messing up.

My perfect life,
A memory gone by.
No more than a dream,
Only pictures to be seen.

Why

2

Why can you not see that I'm hurting.
Why can you not see that I need space.
Why can you not see that I need you.
Why does it feel like you don't understand.
Why does it feel like you don't give a damn.
Why does it always sound like a yell.
Why is it always hell.
Why can't you see me... for me.

The Pain That Runs Deep

You know what it's like to be in pain.
But you don't know what my pain feels like.
It's a crushing weight on my shoulders that never
goes away,
No matter how hard I try to forget.
To forget where I am,
To forget what's going on around me.
This pain stays with me.
It follows me around as if leashed to my body.
It's there when I'm at school,
It's there when I'm at home.
It runs through my veins,
Slowly replacing what keeps me sane.
It's hard to forget,
It's hard to ignore,
This pain that runs deep,
Deeper than my soul.

A Confusion Deeper Than Words

I always ask myself,
'Where is He?'
'Why does He not help me?'
I've always been told to have faith,
But what am I supposed to have faith in?
They say He is always there,
That He will always be there when you need
Him.
There are times that I wonder,
'Did this happen because He wanted it for me?
Or did I make my own destiny?'

This confusion consumes me,
It's all I think about.
I'm surrounded by faith,
But mine is nowhere to be found.
Too much has happened,
To let me believe.
To believe in something more,
Something all-seeing and knowing,
Planning my every move.

But what if there is something out there?
Something benevolent and kind?
This confusion is crippling,
Breaking me from the inside.

Words So Deep

5

The whispered words,
More hurtful than a punch.
They hook deep in my skin,
Straight through to my core.

So deep inside,
No way to expel them.
The words that become,
A part of who I am.

Hidden behind hands,
Spoken in undertones.
Their mouths continue,
To open and close.

The words they use,
Cut deeper than knives.
The words they use,
Full of hate and despise.

Anger

I have an anger inside me,
That runs deep in my veins.
It consumes and controls me,
With no way to escape.

It stems from all roots,
Attacks from all sides.
It feels overwhelming,
Like the incoming tide.

Washing over me,
A wave of emotion.
Wild and fierce,
Unable to deny.

It controls me,
It invades my mind.
It devours my soul,
It disengages me from the world.

Calm

The tide falls,
And the chaos subsides.
There is only silence,
After the storm I derived.

The anger spread,
A blackness in my heart.
Until I found,
A way to block it out.

The cracks slowly healed,
The wounds stitching closed.
My innermost turmoil,
Now calm instead of a storm.

Peace

8

There is a peace in my heart,
A sense of peace in my soul.
My mind is finally quiet,
Thoughts washing over in a gentle roll.

First anger, then calm,
And now there is peace.
A storm washed through,
And now we can breathe.

Making peace with myself,
And with my family too.
Soothing old hurts,
And mending old wounds.

Little by Little

After the storm,
There is peace.
And with peace,
There is understanding.

It may not happen,
In one fell swoop.
But soon enough,
It will come to you.

Little by little,
You will heal.
Little by little,
You will grow.

Little by little,
You will see.
There is a whole wide world,
Just waiting for you to be.

Day by Day

Day by day,
Your heart will grow.
Day by day,
Your eyes will show.

Day by day,
Hour by hour,
Minute by minute,
Second by second.

Day by day,
The hands keep moving.
Day by day,
Time passes by.

Day by day,
You will come to see.
Day by day,
Understanding slowly arrives.

It Gets Easier

It gets easier,
As time goes on.
Life passes by,
People move on.

Understanding and acceptance,
They slowly arrive.
It gets easier,
As life unfolds.

Experiences build,
And collect over time.
A little horde of xp,
To boost you from time to time.

It gets easier,
To move forward and not back.
It gets easier,
To look for the good and not the bad.

One Day

One day I'll get there,
One day I'll reach.
The highest achievement,
Available to me.

Always pushing me,
Go further, do more!
Till one day I believe,
I can do it no more.

I've reached my limit,
My ladder has ended.
I have nothing more to give,
My well has run dry.

One day, maybe,
They'll make up for the cost.
One day, maybe,
I'll recover what I've lost.

Hopes, Dreams, and Everything In Between

There came a day,
When I finally said no.
I stood my ground,
And put my foot down.

I decided to do,
What was best for me.
I decided to hope,
That I could be free.

Engineering or architecture,
Math or science.
Those were my only options,
Apparently.

I could be an author,
But only on the side.
Do something that will make you,
Financially sound.

My brain can't compute,
All the equations and formulas.
I'm just not wired for that,
I finally figured out.

So I switched things around,
Made a few changes.
I dared to hope,
That dreams could be real.

I waited with bated breath,
To find out for sure.
Was it worth taking a chance,
On something that might not occur?

Space More and Less

15

It finally happened,
It finally became real.
I found my true calling,
I found my place in life.

I can become my own person,
Free from assumptions and prying eyes.
The pressure to measure up,
Is no longer a worry of mine.

My mind is at ease,
My worries are appeased.
I pack my belongings,
Preparing for more space.

I no longer had my own bedroom,
And I shared a bathroom with two people more.
Yet somehow I became,
More at home than ever before.

You

When I think of you,
My heart beats fast.
When I see you,
I have a heart attack.

You made me unsteady,
Unsure of myself.
I second-guessed everything,
What I said and how I'd act.

I dressed for you,
And said it's for me.
I made excuses,
To get you to see me.

I float above the trees,
Soar through the clouds.
You lift me up,
When I'm feeling down.

Who You Are To Me

Your smile makes butterflies flutter,
Tickling me with their phantom wings.
Your touch is electricity,
Humming through my veins.

Your warmth surrounds me,
Cozy as a fluffy blanket.
Your arms hold me tight,
Protecting me from what's out of sight.

You are the eye of my storm,
Grounding me with your strength.
You are my super glue,
Piecing me together after I shatter.

You are my life,
You are my love.
You are my rock,
You are my heart.

Unexpected Distance and Closeness

It happened all at once,
It came out of the blue.
We had no way to know,
What distance could do.

We were still really new,
Barely six months through.
Not sure if we'd survive,
This distance that was all so new.

We returned to our homes,
Reunited with our families.
Yet unable to escape,
This closeness we were forced into.

Skype and Snapchat became our new best
friends,
Full of late night calls and mid-day laughs.
The distance was long but the time grew longer,
Until the day I was back in your arms.

Reunited

It wasn't very long,
People would say.
But to me,
It was an eternity.

You came to celebrate,
It was only a short visit.
But days turned to weeks,
And weeks turned to months.

The distance was hard,
We didn't want that again.
So we kept making excuses,
For you to stay near.

Eventually it happened,
My wish came true.
You decided to stay,
And one year became two.

The Little Things

The little things matter,
They count for so much.
Making food or getting coffee,
Out of the love in your heart.

Giving me a hug,
When you know I need it most.
Those forehead kisses,
Always mean the world.

It's the little things you do,
That make my heart melt.
Just as much as the big things,
That show how much you care.

The Everyday Things

The little things make me melt,
But it's the everyday things that make a
difference.
Grocery shopping and doing the dishes,
The unwanted chores that you always lend a
hand with.

It's true that things get messy,
But that's just life.
Coats on the couch and clothes on the floor,
We're both guilty of it all.

But we take care of each other,
And that's the everyday thing that matters most.
At the end of the day as long as I have you,
Everything else in our world could be a mess.

Everything

You are everything to me.
You're there for me,
Day or night,
Good or bad.

You never let me drown,
You never let me get overwhelmed.
Sometimes I wonder if I'm good enough at doing
the same for you,
So I give you my everything.

No matter what happens in life,
I will always stand by your side.
Even when things get messy,
You will never be on your own.

Through late nights and early mornings,
And all the things in between.
I know if I have you then you have me,
And that is everything.

* 9 7 8 9 3 5 7 6 1 7 4 6 8 *